# My Life
# that I Chose
# Myself

*The Eternal Word,*
*the One God, the Free Spirit,*
*Speaks through Gabriele,*
*As through All Prophets of God –*
*Abraham, Moses, Isaiah, Job, Elijah,*
*Jesus of Nazareth, the Christ of God*

Gabriele
Publishing House

First Edition, September 2017
Published by:
© Gabriele Publishing House - The Word
Max-Braun-Str. 2
97828 Marktheidenfeld, Germany
www.gabriele-verlag.com
www.gabriele-publishing-house.com

Original German title:
"Mein Leben, das ich selbst gewählt"

The German edition is the work of reference for all
questions regarding the meaning of the contents
Authorized translation from
Gabriele-Verlag Das Wort GmbH

Printed by: KlarDruck GmbH, Marktheidenfeld, Germany

Order No. S 345en
ISBN 978-3-89201-945-9

# Table of Contents

# Foreword

*"My life" – however it may be – I chose it myself.*

*In a television program, Gabriele, the prophetess and emissary of God for our time, gave explanations and impulses regarding this; they are passed on in this book in written form.*

# My Life,
# that I Chose Myself

A poem, whose message gives us something
to think about: *"The Life that I Chose Myself"*

*Before I came into this earthly life,*
*I was shown how I would live this life.*
*There were the troubles, there was the grief,*
*There was the misery*
*And the burden of suffering.*
*There was the vice that should seize me,*
*There was the delusion that captivated me.*
*There was the quick rage, in which I rampaged,*
*There was hatred, arrogance, pride and shame.*
*But there was also the joy of those days*
*That are filled with light and beautiful dreams,*
*Where neither lamentation nor vexation exist,*
*And everywhere the fount of gifts flows freely.*
*Where love gives the bliss of letting go*
*To the one still bound in the earthly garment.*

*Where the person who escaped the human pain*
*As a chosen one thinks of spirits on high.*

*I was shown the bad and the good,*
*I was shown the fullness of my failings,*
*I was shown the wounds that ran with blood,*
*I was shown the angels' helping deed.*
*And as I so beheld my life to come,*
*I heard a being asking the question:*
*Whether I dared to live this life,*
*For the hour of decision was at hand.*

*So once more I weighed all the bad.*
*"This is the life I want to live!"*
*My answer resounded strong and decisive,*
*And I quietly took on my new fate.*
*And so, I was born into this world,*
*So was it as I entered this new life.*
*I don't lament when often I'm not glad,*
*For I affirmed it when not yet born.* *

* Author unknown, attributed to Hermann Hesse

## "My Life" – the View of the Individual Person – God Does Not Speak about His Personal Life

Dear reader, how often do we hear or talk about our life, for instance: "My life was successful." Or: "There were lots of ups and downs in my life." Or: "I can't really complain about my life." Or even: "My life was a hard life. I was and am often sick." Or: "My life was marked by fate." Or: "In my life I lacked courage and persistence." Or also: "I was often alone in my life; I was lonely and unhappy." Or: "Now my life is coming to an end. My body is worn out and old." Or: "If I could be young again, I would live my life totally differently," etc., etc.

Each person has his own individual life. The range of variations in life, as experienced by the individual person, could be continued without interruption, because each person could report many characteristic details from his life on Earth. Over countless generations, each person had his own life, often according to the respective time, with different degrees of joy and suffering, always provided with a break, through birth and death.

And so, throughout the generations, each person had his life on Earth, and that, right up to this day. And from each and every person we hear that it is his life, in which he believes.

Wouldn't it be strange, if the eternal, universal Spirit, whom we in the western world call God, would speak to us about a personal, heavenly life, instead of the true, the eternal, life? It is the life that continues without interruption, which is the law of the eternal Being, the law of infinity – eternally, because God is eternal, omnipresent law, eternal life.

From the eternal, universal Spirit, we do not hear that it is His personal life. The life, which God, the Eternal, reveals – also in the so-called Bibles, which still contain individual statements of the truth, which is God – is the eternal life. Why does the eternal, universal Spirit, God, speak about eternal life and we human beings talk about our life, about the life of each individual?

An important and decisive question! Why? And so, where does the striking difference come from? – The simple and concise answer is: It is simply a question of consciousness.

## *God Is the Eternally Infinite Life Itself, From Which the Universe Emerged*

Many people do not see the details of their existence in the context of higher dimensions; therefore, they talk about "their life," about "my life." They then speak from the perspective of their human, constricted consciousness. The cosmic consciousness is still closed to many people, because they have not yet completed the steps of spiritual evolution, because they lack an orientation to the Ten Commandments of God and the Sermon on the Mount of Jesus.

The eternal Spirit, God, does not have to be on the lookout for the cosmic, the highest, consciousness, because He is it Himself. He is the All-consciousness, which encompasses everything that is.

God is the law of infinity, the eternal life. From the law of infinity God gave Himself form. Thus, in the Kingdom of God He is the highest spirit being among His sons and daughters, the spirit beings. He is the Father-Mother-God. The Father-Mother-God is also our heavenly Father, because in the innermost part of our soul – in the very basis of our soul – we are spirit beings of the Kingdom of God. Our heavenly Father does not speak about the life of an individual spirit being. At all times, through His messengers, through the prophets and prophetesses, He taught, and teaches, us the unity of life. The life is the eternal, holy law, the Absolute Law, from which all pure forms came, and come, forth.

Through the messengers of the heavens in the Old Testament, God, the Eternal, taught us that life is everlasting. And His Son, Christ, the Redeemer of all souls and people, taught in the New Testament, and teaches again today via the prophetic word, that the eternal life has its order, and that the powers of the eternal Being, of the eternal law, GOD, are in all life forms. It is the holy power of His Order, His Will, His Wisdom, His Earnestness, His Patience, the same as Kindness, His Love and Mercy, the same as Gentleness.

So the words from the Spirit of God are given to us to think about. We should not merely listen or read, but think along with what we hear or read, to grasp what is being said, because it is a part of us; it concerns our true, eternal life.

We are free Christians, people who follow Jesus, the Christ. We do not have an external religion. The inner religion is free. It is the life – in the last analysis, our eternal life. Through our behavior, we chose the life on Earth ourselves. Through the content of our feeling, thinking, speaking and acting, our life on Earth was shaped. And so, we have it in hand ourselves. This is why we are free – free Christians, who decide about their life.

From God's love, from His heart, the spirit beings of heaven emerged and emerge. All the powers of the true, eternal Being are in all life forms; thus, they also exist in each person, in each animal, in all the stars and planets, in all of nature. Because all things form a unity, all the heavenly planes flow into one another as power and light. This also takes place in all divine beings.

As a whole, all powers of the heavens are the law of the Being, the life. Each spirit being is compressed, eternal law, that is, a being in the All-law, which is the life of the spirit being and which permeates it as the breath of God, as life force. The eternal law is the radiation of primordial light, GOD, the eternal life. All planets in all heavenly planes and in all universes are permeated and maintained by the eternal law. They move in their orbits, which are determined by the great helmsman, God, the law. All life forms of the nature kingdoms in the Kingdom of God, of the eternal Being, are oriented to the primordial light, the law of life. It is the immutable love for God and neighbor.

And so, this means that all stars and planets of the Kingdom of God, all spirit beings, all forms of being in the nature kingdoms, are permeated by the eternal primordial light, the eternal law. As in the purely spiritual, light-material Kingdom of God, so is it also in the compressed, part-material worlds and in matter – there, enveloped by the shells that consist of transformed-down divine energy. All universes, all Being – human beings, animals and plants – bear within the All-law, GOD.

Light and power mean unity. Light and power is the consonance of the eternal law of love for God and neighbor. From this, follows that true love is the consonance of the Being that knows no shadows. And, true love is the true, eternal life that is totally bathed in sunshine. And so, life is unity, consensus in all eternity. This is why no spirit being talks about its life, because in the law of God it is the life of eternity. The law of God, the eternal life, is thus also the consonance in all divine beings, and in the nature kingdoms of the Kingdom of God.

## The Person's Responsibility for His Behavior, His Measure of Value, His Becoming – Fateful Consequences, also for His Soul in the Beyond

If we sense and feel into the depths of these brief explanations from the eternal kingdom, the eternal Being, the life, GOD, which is unity, then many a one will realize that the human life, which revolves around "my life," can only be the life of the individual, not the eternal life, the impersonal life of unity, of the love for God and neighbor.

If we would view our life on Earth as a short stage, as a short becoming, then we could better integrate ourselves in the total cosmic context. We would understand and learn what birth and dying signify, for instance, in view of our eternal being. From a higher point of view, we would assign a totally different meaning, a totally different value, to the circumstances and occurrences during the course of our life on Earth.

The value of our earthly existence, of the existence of each and every person, is ultimately determined by each one, himself. He shapes it by way of his behavior toward his fellow people, toward the animals, plants and the whole Earth.

A person's behavior patterns are the result of his feelings, his sensations, thoughts, his words and actions, of everything that he feels, thinks, speaks and does, day after day. This then becomes the imprint of his body, and he gradually becomes this. This is, then, the human being, and accordingly, his soul. And so, what a person does in the way of what is good and God-pleasing for the benefit of his body and his soul, or expects of it in the way of what is less good, that is, bad, that is what he calls "his life."

A person's life on Earth consists of his personal inputs, of what he thinks and says, and his views, for example, his concept of rights and of being right, even to his concept of justice. Over the years, his individual personality develops from this, which can also be called the person-law, because it is tailored to the person, to his personal aspects. This is, then, the person's personal measure of value, which determines his behavior and his personal development, that is, becoming. This is what he calls "my life."

Since the individual person shapes and determines his becoming with his specific inputs into his body and soul, according to the causal law, this brings about consequences. This results in what the person on Earth and his soul in the soul realms have to learn – or also to suffer. This is the law of "action equals reaction," also called the "law of cause and effect" or "sowing and reaping," in short, the causal law.

## The Causal Law – Counterbalancing Principle in the Pros and Cons of the Earthly Existence and the "Beyond"

According to the law "action equals reaction," or "sowing and reaping," each person always reaps solely what he himself has input as seeds into his body and into his soul. The manifold events of his seed and of his harvest are what he then calls "his life." From this personal becoming of pros and cons, joy and sorrow develop in the course of his earthly existence. This is logically comprehensible, but many a one would like to refuse to accept the fact that he is responsible for his fate, hardship and illness. He has to finally realize that solely those bad things hit him, which correspond to his personal inputs. And so, each person himself determines his course of becoming, which he calls "his life." Nevertheless, we may not overlook the fact that the cosmic universal life, however, is not meant here, but solely the occurrences and contingencies of his earthly existence, which he – as stated – determines himself.

The divine, the eternally infinite pure Being, the life of the heavens, on the other hand, is unalterable and exempt from the grasp of the wanting, egoistical, narrow-minded human being. Since the All-law, God, the Absolute, is good, through and through, what is wanted and desired in a human way and that corresponds to self-will and egoism, can therefore be only not good – that is, unlawful, or, bad and harmful.

The human body can also be described as the temporary garment of the soul. This statement implies the question: What will happen after the person's course of becoming, when his garment falls away. Where will the person's soul be, then?

One answer could be that each day the person sets the course for the journey of his soul, which slips out of the now rigid physical body and is drawn to that region of the beyond where energies of unresolved guilt are waiting for it. It is those burdens and bindings from which the person could and should have liberated his soul via self-recognition and clearing them up while incarnated. And so, each day, each person determines where the soul will be after the death of his body.

For a deeper understanding, another image: The human being can be compared to a computer. Virtually every day, each of us enters data into the computer "human being." Person and soul store the respective inputs, but corresponding planetary constellations also absorb the data of each and every person, and very gradually, day by day, radiate it to the soul and the person. The person successively experiences such corresponding inputs, that is, data, which he had previously input over the course of his earthly existence. Likewise, the planetary constellations also stimulate the discarnate soul to face up to this and to clear up what the discarded garment, the person, thought and spoke toward it over the course of its incarnation. And so, the soul is confronted with the negative inputs of its former person and faces the task of unraveling these energy knots of what is not good.

Independent of whether, we reap joy or sorrow based on our inputs – we should be aware of one thing: What is decisive for our present and future destiny is the degree of our selflessness and neighborly love. As long as the person strives to be his own neighbor, as long as he presents himself and acts accordingly, he records causes after causes. With this egocentric attitude, many a one – proverbially – "stops at nothing."

## *For or Against God –*
## *Love for God and Neighbor*
## *or the Satanic*
## *"I Myself Am My Own Neighbor"?*

Jesus of Nazareth taught us the law of freedom, which is based on love for God and neighbor, and not on self-love, not on egomania, and which is dismissed so concisely with "I myself am my own neighbor." This kind of egoism is in direct contrast to love for God and neighbor.

The law of freedom, which Jesus of Nazareth taught us, says that each person is himself responsible for his way of thinking and behaving, according to the principle acknowledged by human beings of "action equals reaction," the law of cause and effect. According to the universal law, this means: Either for God, the eternal life, or against God, the eternal life.

The one who is against the law of freedom of life has reversed the statement of love for God and neighbor into "I myself am my own neighbor." So from this reversal of love for God and neighbor, very gradually the satanic developed: "I myself am my own neighbor," which is based on bondage and on being bound to obedience, according to the principle: "Bind, and be your own neighbor." Under this attitude, which is based solely on self-love, not only do people suffer, but above all, the innocent animals, the plants, the minerals, the whole Earth.

At some point, and be it in the beyond as a soul or, newly incarnated in a human body in future incarnations, the soul has to face its inputs, that is, its personal responsibility. And so, we, each one of us, are subject to our own servitude, which can express itself as sorrow, worry, hardship, illness and further dissonances.

## *Grasping and Fathoming the Impulses from the Energy of the Day*

Where could we start to find our way out of this sorrowful carousel, the pitfall of fear about what our life on Earth might surely bring to us? The beginning, which literally shakes us awake to self-recognition, is always our day, the day of each individual. The day clearly points out what we have burdened our body and our soul with in the past, that is, which information we have input into our body, into the cells of our body and into our soul. Each day brings us a part of this, so that we work off what otherwise could at some point painfully hit us.

Have a care! Today the day may start out cheerfully. With the so-called sunshine in our feelings, we think it will be a day with many good sides for us. Then we may talk about balance and happiness: "Today is a good day. My mood is happy and cheerful." But several hours later, the picture suddenly changes. For example, we meet a former work colleague and strike up a conversation. Very casually he or she mentions a situation relating to a former mutual activity. Suddenly the cheerful mood sinks. A touch of bad-temper, even depression, is in the making. The conversation has the effect of a cloudbank that covers over the cheerful feelings. What was that? Was it a hint from our personal energy of the day? Since, as we know, nothing happens by chance, the conversation was certainly a pointer at something that we once input in the so-called computer soul and person, since soul and person are, as mentioned, memory banks that record everything that we sense, feel, think, speak and do. Now it is up to us to question this see-saw of emotions that has been set into motion and that triggered a kind of jumble of thoughts going to and fro: What does the day want to tell us? What lies in the memory banks consciousness and sub-conscious and also in our soul, that is, what a planetary constellation stored and radiates to us today, that is, now? – What is it?

If you believe in the universal Spirit, whom we in the western world call GOD, then trust and pray to the Spirit of God, who is the universal law of love for God and neighbor. Ask for support and help. If we honestly ask from our heart, we should also take enough time, perhaps in the evening, as soon as things have calmed down, when the day with its many activities fades away and turns into evening. Some distance from the daily occurrences opens up our mind, so that we suddenly have an "aha" experience, because an inkling rises that conveys to us why a hint of depression clouded our good mood.

Jesus, the Christ, taught us: "Ask, and it will be given to you. Seek and you shall find. Knock and it will be opened to you." God, who is the All-life, knows us, because He is our heavenly Father.

God, the Spirit of our heavenly Father, is present in us. He is the life. He knows about our worries and hardships and supports us in our hour of distress, if we rely on Him and trust that He is the helmsman of all that is good.

Perseverance is the path to Him, God in us. Precisely at that point in time when we can grasp what is the best for us, it flows to us –

perhaps early in the morning or in a situation during the day, or in the evening. Whenever we are able to easily grasp it, we sense and experience what God wants to tell us. The "aha" experience is a kind of dawning of thoughts and pictures from which we can recognize what our dejection or depression is all about. In any case, we have stored something in our soul as well as in our physical body, from which the soul wants to liberate itself before its shell, the person, has to endure the effects of these inputs.

Our day has many pointers. In numerous situations during the day, it wants to bring home to us what we should question and correct. It, the day, is well-disposed toward us; it warns us in good time.

Everything, but absolutely everything, is energy. Everything that we emit is energy, which, according to the pros and cons of our way of thinking, speaking and acting, is recorded and at some point comes to us, often bit by bit. And so, what we have stored in the many, many days of our earthly existence, the pros and cons, are part of our course of becoming as a person or of the journey of our soul after the death of our body.

*Make Use of Your Days on Earth!*
*The Manifestation of the Power of God in*
*Nature Speaks of Unity,*
*of Love for God and Neighbor*

The day, our day, is a good friend. The Spirit of God, our Father, always strives to have us recognize in time, through our day, what still exists in the way of not good aspects, so that we may correct it before what we call a fate-filled life breaks in over us in our physical body – or, after we pass on, in the soul. Each day, we are frequently stimulated to recognize ourselves in the bad situations, to learn from them, so that we direct our course of becoming as a human being onto the pathways of eternal life in time, so that our soul has a so-called "ascension" before it, as soon as it discards its shell, the physical body.

If the person does not make use of his days on Earth and, despite all his deep recognitions, allows his thoughts, his whole behavior to be uncontrolled, then after the death of the body the soul will set out again on its journey in the soul realms, according to its burdens, which the person inflicted on it through his behavior. And what can develop from such a soul journey? Perhaps a fall to Earth in a future incarnation. The soul, which has then slipped into a new earthly body, has again taken up its course of becoming as a human being. The new person with his inputs from previous lives then calls his new, that is, old, blows of fate "his hard life." The journeys of the soul and perhaps further incarnations of the soul in a human body will continue until soul and person awaken to the awareness of what life truly means.

The Almighty Spirit, God, who is the life, is unity. He is the Father of all His children, including us human beings. He, God, is the Creator of all Being. He is the life in everything. In every stone, in every drop of water, in nature, in every animal and, as we hear again and again, in every soul, in every person, is God, the life. In the elements, in everything that the Earth carries is the life. The life is the breath of life, God, in the breath of the person. Everything lives because God is the life. Everything bears immortality within, because life is everlasting.

Let us become aware once more that God, the Father of all His children, is the Creator of all Being. He manifests Himself in everything with the words of revelation, "I Am the I Am, the life." And so, God is unity. God is love for His entire Creation. Love for God and neighbor is the manifestation of life in the minerals, in all plants, in each animal. In all the diversity of nature, is the universal Spirit, God; it is the life. And so, life is unity, and thus, love for God and neighbor.

The person, who talks about "his life" and believes he is the "crown of creation" vegetates away in his "I myself am my own neighbor," which he calls his life and considers as his crown. Under this, his crown, he murders, kills and rapes, he proves himself to be the robber of the natural world of plants and the murderer and butcher of the animal world, which, in the end, he even consumes. Just as the lust-driven fellow, the person, acts – as the so-called "crown of creation" – he thinks he is entitled to take the life of nature and the animals. He, the driven fellow, the driven perpetrator, is of the opinion that the life of evolution, which is the breath of God in nature and in the animal world, is inferior, because this allegedly "inferior life" has no feelings, compared to the so-called "crown of creation," the human being.

*Reverence for Life – Do Feelings and Conscience Still Exist? The Boundless Brutalization of the Human Being*

With all that today's society offers, the question arises: Does the alleged crown of creation, the human being, still have the feelings that contribute to the formation of conscience? Let's start with the emotions of a hunter, for instance: The hunter chases creatures of God, the animals, through the woods and over the fields, shooting them down "gun-happy" – so, he kills them. The weapon is thus a substitute for feelings and the formation of conscience. The "crown of creation," which the hunter believes he is, takes the animal's life. The question is: Did he, the human being, give life to the animal – or did the Creator, the true, eternal crown, which is the life? The satanic huntsman's call is: "I myself am my own neighbor!" This is the compulsiveness of the human ego, which has nothing to do with forming feelings and a conscience, but at best, with maudlin sentimentality, when he sits at the beer table and boasts about how many animals he has shot.

Many an ego show-off is either Catholic or Protestant Lutheran, or designates himself as belonging to another religion. What could the so-called "Saint" Jerome give him to understand, who wrote: *The eating of flesh was unknown until the deluge. But after the deluge, the poison of flesh-meat was offered to our teeth ... But once Christ has come in the end of time, and Omega passed into Alpha and turned the end into the beginning, we are no longer allowed to eat flesh."*

However, the Catholic Church, which canonized the Doctor of the Church, Jerome, even puts on "Masses in honor of St. Hubert," to bless the carcasses of wantonly killed animals. Isn't that a mockery of its "saint"?

The human being, who has turned into a killing machine, where human being, animal, nature and even Mother Earth are concerned, calls his compulsive, human course of becoming his "life." It continues in a similar vein with the so-called "unfortunate life," of which the failed crown of creation is even proud. The human being, who in the satanic statement "I myself am my own neighbor," presents himself as the crown of creation, keeps so-called slaughter animals, which, from the outset, are destined for the butcher. The killing machinery begins already in barns that are unworthy of animals. When the livestock is ready for slaughter, then it is handed over to the butcher's bolt gun. The butcher in the slaughterhouse clubs or shoots, that is, murders the animal. Its carcass is hung and slit open, depending on how big it is, either with the corresponding saw or with a butcher knife.

Here, the question to the so-called keeper of slaughter animals and to the butcher: Did you give life to the animals, since you allow yourselves to take their lives?
God, who is the life, did not allow you this. He is the Creator of the animals. He is the giver of life. And so, who allowed you this? Who!?
The unconscionable, compulsive one, who is against God's creation, the satan in the

unfeeling, driven perpetrator, is the animal murderer of all God's creatures, but also the murderer of the plant world, because God is the life in all of nature.

The brutalization of the human social machine knows no limits. Let us bring to mind the hunted and chased animals, which in the woods and fields were, and are, killed with a gun or beaten with a club. Or let us put ourselves in the place of the tortured creatures that are tormented and tortured because of their flesh, which were, and are, mostly kept as slaughter animals in unworthy barns, to then be taken to the butcher. In the situation in which their life is violently taken, they are all afraid. The animals' cries of fear and their murderous death go on the account of the souls of the animal torturers and murderers, and of those who condone such things.

The flesh of the animal carcasses, cut up into portions, then ends up at the meat counters of the butcher shops and supermarkets. The consumer, who indulges in animal cannibalism, purchases a piece of meat full of suffering from the killing machine and takes it, tastefully prepared, to be eaten at the table. The person, who describes his life as "the life," and grandly calls himself the "crown of creation," cuts it up, if at all, on his plate with knife and fork or bites off the prepared piece of carcass lying on a piece of bread or tears it, gnawing it from the bone. This is then the "course of values" of the person, who characterizes as "his life" that which is based on the satanic statement "I myself am my own neighbor!" Everyone who consumes pieces of animal carcasses also shares in the guilt according to the statement of Jerome, whom the Church canonized, but whose teaching, however, it does not respect.

Animal cannibalism is becoming ever more common, because the feeling for life has been lost and thus, the formation of conscience, as well. The tools of torture and killing have many names. The latter are called, among others: rifle, pistol, club, bolt, etc., etc. The torture is in keeping slaughter animals and then the passage to the butcher. As already mentioned, the cut-up trophies then come to the table roasted and spiced for the animal cannibals. This is then what the human being calls "his life." From this, among other things, is deduced the motto: "I myself am my own neighbor!"

The ecclesiastical-traditional spirits of confusion, which many people believe in, have – as already mentioned – reversed Jerome's clear statement into its opposite. In addition, they have made their faithful believe that animals have no souls, no feelings, and that plants are merely matter without life. More animals suffer as a result of this whitewashing, which is the order of the black ranks.

As their brothers and sisters, they, too, are massacred, and their pelt, which is skinned, is processed to serve the so-called "beauties," whose meaning of life is, among other things, to shine with fur hats, fur capes, fur coats and the like, in the hope that this way they would be the most beautiful. However, before the pelt of the animal was tanned, that is, processed, they were caught in cruel traps or had to vegetate away on so-called "fur farms," a lifelong hell in small wire cages.

This is how the human dynasty of corpses decorates what it calls "its life."

The many, many animal species in the oceans, on and in the Earth and in the air call to their Creator for help. And fishing – that is, overfishing – in the world oceans for the benefit of "I myself am my own neighbor," is a part of the murder of the animal world.

Whether spring, summer, autumn or winter, at the convenience of the lustful nature killers, trees can be cut down all year long, because according to the ecclesiastical-traditional spirits of confusion, plants, like animals, are not ensouled life. The Earth, seen as a whole, is thus at the mercy of the plunderers and robbers, because the said teaching dismisses all life forms as inanimate objects, with the exception of the so-called promising "crown of creation," which long ago already dedicated itself to the underworld, to the "doom-mongering," and has become servile to their promptings. These well-positioned ruling ranks taught and teach that the human being should subdue the Earth. He did and does that – in his brutal way.

Now the Earth with all its living beings and life forms is calling for help and rescue. When the elements of the Earth then come to help, in which, among other things, also the saver of life, the life, is effective, the human infamous deeds, the atrocities, are even attributed to God and declared to be the so-called "mysteries of God."

*The Time Is Ripe;*
*the Truth Comes to Light.*
*People Who Have Found Their Way*
*to the Awareness of the True Life*
*Will Be an Example for Many*

Now the time is ripe, in which the opponent of God gains less and less foothold on the Earth, because the Earth is and remains God's footstool, which cannot be destroyed, even when the church-traditional clan accuses God ever so often. The devilish-murderous game with the notion of being able to defeat God is gradually coming to an end. The "white-washers" bear witness of themselves, of who they are, more and more often. Ever more people are recognizing that what formerly presented itself as white is gradually turning out to be black.

When the temporary garment of the soul falls away, that is, when the person passes on, the driven perpetrator, the murderer of the animals and of nature, who has unscrupulously wreaked havoc on Earth, must recognize as a soul what life means and who the life is. All the slaughtered animals in, on and over the Earth, that is, all the animals in woods and fields, as well as the slaughter animals and the animals in the waters, but also the animals in laboratories, will one day rise up in the soul as pictures of suffering and horror. The soul cannot escape these pictures, for it was the cruel deed of the person, which he entered into his soul and into those planetary constellations that are now the soul's present dwelling places.

Many a soul in the beyond thinks: "I will now free myself from these torments and go into another incarnation." However, before the soul, which has stored these cruel deeds, incarnates, it is taught. It is taught about everything that will happen to it. The poem cited at the beginning, "The Life I Chose Myself" comes alive in it and it has to finally recognize that its former life on Earth as a human being, which is recorded in it, can one day come to it again. In a new human existence, a part of the former inputs will come into effect, according to the law: Whatever a person sows, he will reap.

So, come what may: The soul, which is again a human being, brought along what has not been expiated. At some point, the days arrive in which a part of the seed presses to be harvested. One can only hope that – if the human shell has reached its degree of maturity – the person will not continue as in its previous incarnations. In any case, these causes will break out some time or other, either in the soul in the soul realms, or in the soul in one of the newly assumed physical bodies.

Happy the person who during his course of becoming as a human being on the Earth makes use of the time! Happy the person who recognizes in time the ecclesiastical-traditional "whitewashers," to whom the person may have been subject, and learns from this! With the help of the Christ of God, he can develop remorse and attain the request for forgiveness. Then he will resist the renewed promptings, by no longer doing what is not good.

People who master their life on Earth in this awareness will contribute to more and more people escaping from the black magic and walking the path of remorse and of clearing up their guilt. They orient themselves more and more to the commandments of God and to the teachings of the great teacher of Wisdom, Jesus, the Christ, to His Sermon on the Mount, which is the path to higher values. In this way, they recognize the true life and find their way to the love for God and neighbor, which is the unity of life, to which belong the animals, nature, the elements, yes, all of life on, in and over the Earth. The life is God. He alone, God, is the giver of life.

Only the human being allows himself to deny people the life, to take the life of animals and nature using cruel ways and means. Who is the driven perpetrator against animals and nature? It is the one who is against the giver of life, God. It is the black magic, which deceptively presents everything dark as white. The call of many people who have found their way to recognition is: O human being, wake up, before your soul discards its shell, for the law of sowing and reaping will become effective at some time or other. Examine, O human being, what your seed, your sowing, is called, for that will one day be your harvest. – This holds true for all of us.

The day of each person is a guide, a pointer, for good, less good, even bad or evil. Each day comes to each one with what the planetary constellations radiate to the person via the soul.

Dear reader, we wish you and all of us a conscious course of becoming in the earthly existence. We are all brothers and sisters in the Spirit of the universal life, God, whom we also address as "Father" in the Lord's Prayer. He is the Creator of life, who is solely the life.

*Read also ...*

# The Path of Forgetting
# The Microcosm
# in the Macrocosm

The truth about each one of us lies in the stars, actually, the heavenly bodies know each one of us through and through … How can we understand this?

In this book we will be led into the lawful principles of life in a very unique way, and this will open up in us new dimensions of our existence. Universal correlations between the microcosm and the macrocosm are explained in such a way that they encompassingly convey the lawful processes that lie behind all life.

Gabriele explains how everything that we as human beings feel, think, speak and do, is not only continually recorded in the microcosm "man," but is also in constant communication with further memory sources in the coarse-material macrocosm and, beyond that, in a finer-material macrocosm. Whoever not only reads the contents of this book, but also thinks about it and relates it to everything that he encounters at every moment, will find that new knowledge opens up to him, the far-reaching significance, which is of unspeakable value for shaping his life.

112 pp., Soft-bound, $8.00, Order No. S 348en

ISBN: 978-3-89201-807-0

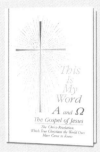

# This Is My Word
## A & Ω
The Gospel of Jesus
The Christ Revelation,
Which True Christians
the World Over
Have Come to Know

A book that allows you to get to know Jesus, the Christ. The truth about His works and life as Jesus of Nazareth.

**From the Table of Contents**: The childhood and youth of Jesus • The falsification of the teachings of Jesus of Nazareth during the past 2000 years • Purpose and meaning of life on Earth • Jesus taught the law of sowing and reaping • Prerequisites for healing the body • Jesus teaches about marriage • The Sermon on the Mount • About the nature of God • God does not get angry or punish • The teaching of "eternal damnation" is a mockery of God • Jesus exposes the scribes and Pharisees as hypocrites • Jesus loved the animals and always stood up for them • The one who lives in God is one with all creatures • The human being violates and destroys the life on Earth • The extinction of many species of animals • The law of sowing and reaping also holds true in dealing with creation • Selfless love, the key to understanding and helping one's neighbor and to insight into the causal law and overcoming it • About death, reincarnation and life • Equality of men and women • The true meaning of the Redeemer-deed of Christ … and much, much more.

With a short autobiography of Gabriele, the prophetess and emissary of God for this time that includes a charcoal drawing of her.

1194 pp., Soft-Bound, $15.00, Order No. S 007en

ISBN: 978-1-890841-38-6

The Contemporary, DEATH

## Living and Dying in Order to Keep Living

Everyone Dies
for Himself Alone

Who doesn't want to find the way out of the fear of death? The author of this book writes the following: "Whoever learns to understand his life will no longer fear death."

Gabriele extensively informs the reader about until now unknown correlations between life and death, about the condition and state of the soul during the whole process of dying in all the different situations it faces, and about what awaits the soul of a person "over there," in the beyond, after the demise of its physical body.

144 pages, Softbd.,
$14.00, Order No. S 368en
ISBN 978-1-890841-35-5

What should have been kept
hidden from you:

## Reincarnation

Life's Gift of Grace

Where Does the Journey
of My Soul Go?

The questions of mankind on "where from" and "where to" have seldom been answered so clearly and unequivocally as by Gabriele, the teaching prophetess and emissary of God for our time.

Learn how the ancient knowledge of mankind that was still alive in early Christianity about the reincarnation of souls was suppressed by the emerging church of power – with fatal consequences until today ...

80 pages, Softbd.,
$7.00, Order No. S 380en
ISBN: 978-1-890841-64-5

We will be happy to send you our free catalog
Gabriele Publishing House – The Word
P.O. Box 2221, Deering, NH 03244, USA

info@gabriele-publishing-house.com